BINARY NUMBERS

Computers have recently brought binary numbers into the public eye, but they have been important to mathematicians for a long, long time before then.

Thousands of years ago the man who invented the game of chess knew how quickly the doubling numbers in the binary-number sequence grow. This book tells how he used his knowledge to ask for a great reward for his invention.

The book also shows the reader how to write numbers in the binary-number sequence and how to write binary numerals themselves. Once the young mathematician learns these principles, he or she will begin to understand how computers can work—and also will be able to write messages in a secret binary numeral code.

BINARY NUMBERS

By Clyde Watson

Illustrated by Wendy Watson

THOMAS Y. CROWELL COMPANY   NEW YORK

YOUNG MATH BOOKS

Edited by Dr. Max Beberman, Director of the Committee on School Mathematics Projects, University of Illinois

Edited by Dorothy Bloomfield, Mathematics Specialist, Bank Street College of Education

Library of Congress Cataloging in Publication Data: Watson, Clyde. Binary numbers (A Young math book). SUMMARY: Introduces the principle and uses of binary numbers. 1. Binary system (Mathematics)—Juv. lit. [1. Binary system (Mathematics) 2. Mathematics] I. Watson, Wendy, illus. II. Title. QA141.4.W37   513'.52   75-29161   ISBN 0-690-00992-5   ISBN 0-690-00993-3 (CQR).

1 2 3 4 5 6 7 8 9 10

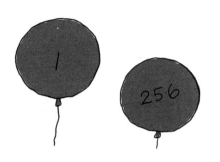

BINARY NUMBERS

Take a ball of string and a ruler. Measure off 1 foot of string and pinch the 1-foot mark between your thumb and index finger. (Mark it with a felt pen if you want to.)

1

Now double this length of string. To do this, fold the string at the 1-foot mark. Make a new mark even with the loose end. Pinch the new mark between thumb and finger, and then straighten out the new length.

How long is the new length? Measure and see.

Double the length again. How many feet long is it now? Guess before you measure. Were you right?

You started with 1 foot. After doubling you had 2 feet, then 4, then 8.   1, 2, 4, 8, ? What number comes next? Make a guess, then fold the string, mark it, lay it out, and measure. Were you right?

Every time you fold the string, the new length is twice the one before it. When you folded the 8-foot piece, the new length was 16 feet, because 8 + 8 (or 8 doubled) is 16. How long a piece will you have if you double the 16-foot length? Guess, try it, then measure. Were you right?

(By now your piece of string is probably too long for the room you're in, so you will have to go outdoors or into a long hall.)

How many times do you think you can double the length before you run out of string? Try it!

If you had a very big ball of string, how many times do you think you could double the length before it went all the way around the earth?

Only 27 doublings would be more than enough.

Can you believe that after only 31 doublings your
string would be long enough to reach to the moon
and beyond?

Take a piece of paper, and do the string-folding trick again, but this time write down how many feet of string you get with each doubling. Before you double, you have 1 foot, so you can write

0	doublings	$\longrightarrow$	1 foot
1	doubling	$\longrightarrow$	2 feet
2	doublings	$\longrightarrow$	4 feet
3	doublings	$\longrightarrow$	8 feet
4	doublings	$\longrightarrow$	?
5	doublings	$\longrightarrow$	?
6	doublings	$\longrightarrow$	?

This set of numbers, 1, 2, 4, 8, 16, 32, 64, . . . has a special name: the **binary number sequence**. Each number is twice the number before it, and the dots after the 64 show that the sequence goes on forever. You can double numbers in the sequence over and over to get a number twice as big each time, just as you can double your length of string over and over to make it twice as long each time.

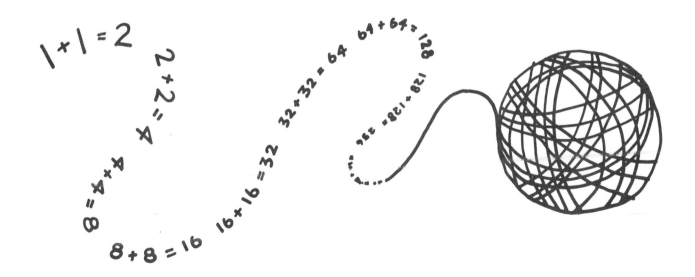

1 + 1 = 2
2 + 2 = 4
4 + 4 = 8
8 + 8 = 16
16 + 16 = 32
32 + 32 = 64
64 + 64 = 128
128 + 128 = 256

An old story tells how pleased the king of India was when he learned the game of chess. He called the inventor of the game before him and said, "As a reward for inventing this wonderful game, I will give you anything you ask for."

The inventor thought for a moment and then he said to the king, "This is what I want for my reward: 1 grain of wheat on the first square of the chessboard, 2 grains of wheat on the second square, 4 grains on the third, 8 on the fourth, and so on for all 64 squares. Each square must hold twice as many grains of wheat as the one before it."

"Is that all you want?" asked the king in surprise. "What a fool!" Then he began to put grains of wheat on the chessboard. What do you think would happen if you tried this?

Just like the lengths of string in the doubling trick, the grains of wheat on the squares of the chessboard would increase very quickly, like this:

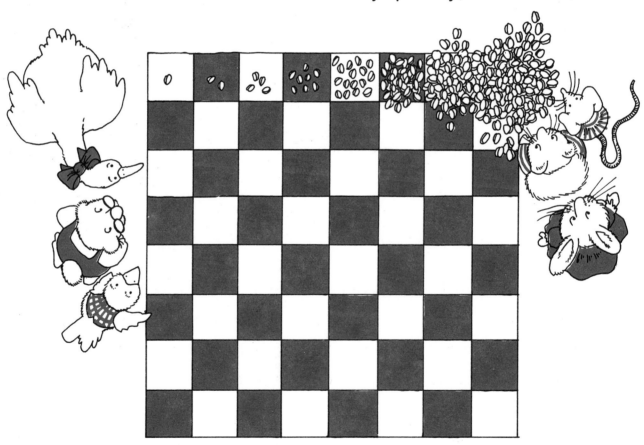

The sixty-fourth and last square would have more than 9,000,000,000,000,000,000 (nine quintillion) grains of wheat on it, and altogether the chessboard would have enough wheat on it to cover the whole earth with a blanket of wheat.

Do you think the inventor got what he asked for?

Along the edge of a piece of cardboard, mark and cut out a strip 1 centimeter wide.

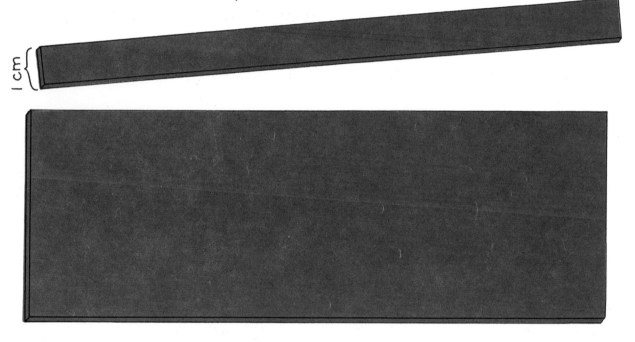

1 cm

(Here is a centimeter ruler. You can use it to measure off your strips.)

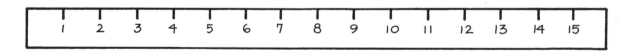

1 2 3 4 5 6 7 8 9 10 11 12 13 14 15

Now mark your strip into four shorter strips: 1 centimeter (1 cm), 2 cm, 4 cm, and 8 cm long. Cut these pieces out and label each one with its length.

(If you have Cuisenaire rods, you can use them instead. Use one white, one red, one purple, and one brown.)

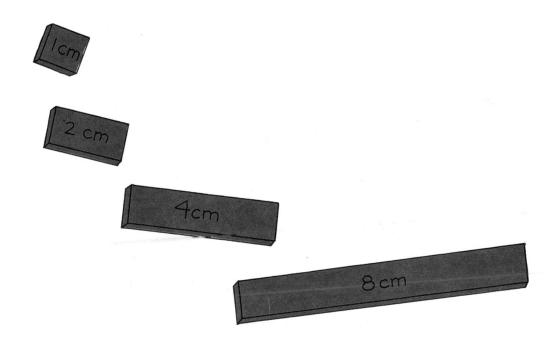

On the ruler drawn on this page, see if you can build lengths for all of the numbers up to 15 using your four strips.

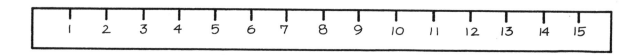

One you can make with the 1-strip. **Two** is also easy: Just use the 2-strip. What about **three**? Is there any way to build **three** using your strips end to end?

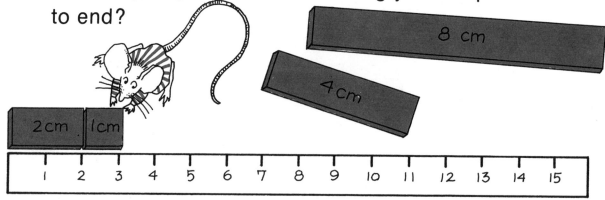

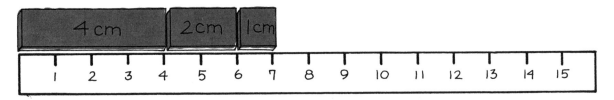

As you build with these four lengths, you will discover something very special about binary numbers. By adding together certain numbers from the sequence, you can build any number you wish. Can you believe that using only the first ten numbers of this sequence you can build numbers all the way up to 1,023?

$8 + 2 + 1 = 11$

$4 + 1 = 5$

$16 + 8 + 1 = 25$

$4 + 2 = 6$

$32 + 8 + 1 = 41$

$16 + 4 + 2 = 22$

$4 + 2 = 6$

$8 + 4 + 1$

Some stores still use a balance with weights to measure things like sugar, flour, rice, fruit, and candy. If a customer asks for one ounce of peppermints, the grocer puts a 1-ounce weight on one side of the balance and a bag for the peppermints on the other. Then he starts filling the bag. When the bag of peppermints and the 1-ounce weight balance perfectly, he knows they weigh the same.

But what if someone wanted eleven ounces of peppermints? Do you think the grocer has eleven 1-ounce weights, or an 11-ounce weight? Probably not. In fact, with just these four weights

1 oz
2 oz
4 oz
8 oz

he could weigh out any amount in ounces up to 15 ounces.

Which weights would he use to weigh out

5 ounces of chocolates?

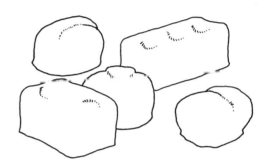

10 ounces of lemon drops?

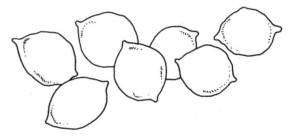

7 ounces of peanuts?

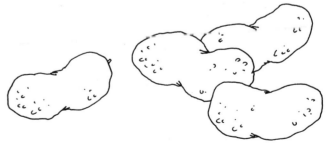

By adding four more weights

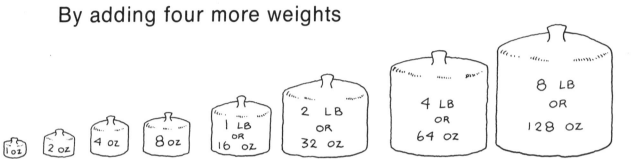

he could weigh out any amount in pounds and ounces up to 15 pounds and 15 ounces. How would he weigh out 3 pounds of cherries?

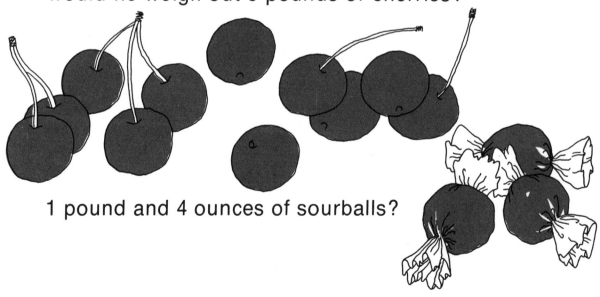

1 pound and 4 ounces of sourballs?

Look in the picture. Can you tell how much the sack of potatoes weighs?

Now you are ready to learn how to write binary numerals. You will need the number strips you made, and a sheet of paper. Write the numbers 1 to 15 down the left-hand side of the page. Across the top, draw a picture of your four strips, in this order: 8, 4, 2, 1. Then write down which strips you need to build each number.

To go beyond 15,
add a 16-column to
the left of the
8-column. Now you
can build numbers up
to 31 before you
need another column.

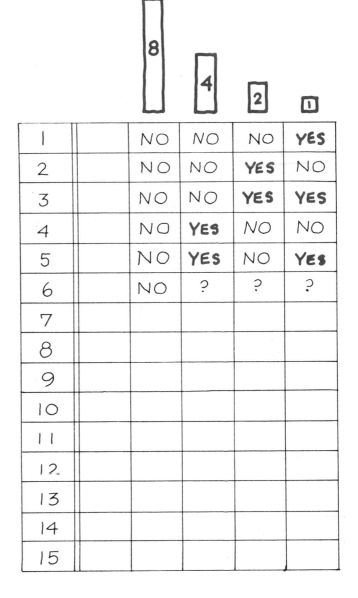

			8	4	2	1
1			NO	NO	NO	YES
2			NO	NO	YES	NO
3			NO	NO	YES	YES
4			NO	YES	NO	NO
5			NO	YES	NO	YES
6			NO	?	?	?
7						
8						
9						
10						
11						
12						
13						
14						
15						

Notice that you have to use only two symbols, **yes** and **no**. Because the binary number system uses only two symbols, it is very handy for computers. Computers work with numbers, sending signals through many electronic switches. Each switch can be either **on** or **off**. Just as you can write any number you please with **yes** and **no**, the computer can "think" any number by turning different switches **on** and **off**.

Think of it this way: You could set up a row of
light bulbs and write numbers with them. Each
bulb would stand for a number in the binary
sequence, just as the strips did:

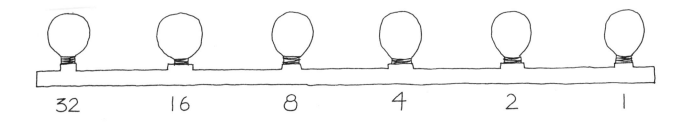

For whatever number you wanted to write, you
would turn certain bulbs **on** and others **off**. On
would mean **yes** and off would mean **no**. The
number five would look like this:

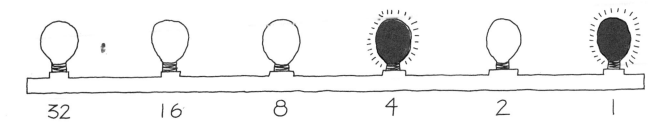

Can you tell what number this is?

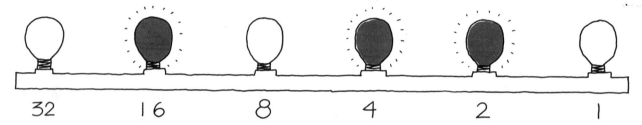

| 32 | 16 | 8 | 4 | 2 | 1 |

It's easier to write numerals than to draw light bulbs or to write yes and no all the time, so mathematicians use **1** for yes (or on) and **0** for no (or off).

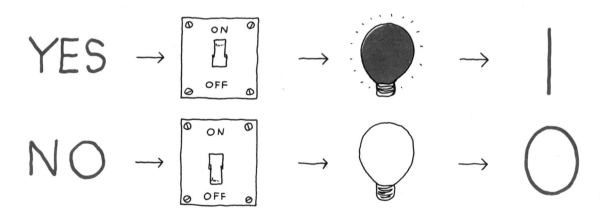

Using your yes and no chart, see if you can write the numbers 1 to 15 with **1**'s and **0**'s. Then turn the page to check yourself.

You don't need to write down the **0**'s in front of the first **1**, but the first **1** and everything after it must stay. And don't read **10** as "ten," read it as "one-zero" because as a binary numeral, **10** means "two."

OOIO = IO

I AND O

	8	4	2	I
I				I
2			I	O
3			I	I
4		I	O	O
5		I	O	I
6				
7				
8				
9				
IO				
II				
12				
13				
14				
15				

Decimal Numerals · Binary Numerals

1	1
2	1 0
3	1 1
4	1 0 0
5	1 0 1
6	1 1 0
7	1 1 1
8	1 0 0 0
9	1 0 0 1
10	1 0 1 0
11	1 0 1 1
12	1 1 0 0
13	1 1 0 1
14	1 1 1 0
15	1 1 1 1

You probably know this code:

A = 1	E = 5	I = 9	M = 13	Q = 17	U = 21	Y = 25
B = 2	F = 6	J = 10	N = 14	R = 18	V = 22	Z = 26
C = 3	G = 7	K = 11	O = 15	S = 19	W = 23	
D = 4	H = 8	L = 12	P = 16	T = 20	X = 24	

You can write secret messages using a binary number code. Translate that code into binary numerals:

A = 1	E = 101	I = 1001
B = 10	F = 110	J = 1010
C = 11	G = 111	K = 101
D = 100	H = 1000	

Then write messages. Do you know what this says?

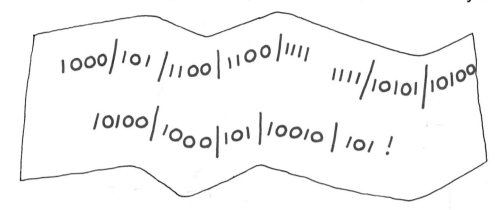

1000/101 /1100|1100|1111   1111/10101|10100

10100/1000|101|10010 | 101 !

How about this?

10011 | 101 | 101   11001|1111 | 10101

1100|1 |10100|101 | 10010,

1|1100 | 1100 /1001 |111 | 1 |10100/1111/10010....

ABOUT THE AUTHOR

Clyde Watson is well known as an author of fiction and poetry for children. In this, her first Young Math Book, her knowledgeable imagination has taken her into a new field.

Ms. Watson has been a teacher in several elementary schools and has concentrated on mathematics activities that have included teaching math in combination with art, music, and even creative writing. She has also held a math laboratory workshop for teachers about working with the latest mathematics materials and with everyday objects.

Clyde Watson now lives in Lyme, New Hampshire.

ABOUT THE ARTIST

Wendy Watson is the well-known illustrator of nearly forty books, many of which have won distinguished awards for their graphic excellence. BINARY NUMBERS is the second book she has illustrated for the Young Math series, but it is also the fifth book she has collaborated on with her sister Clyde. Born and raised in Putney, Vermont, Wendy Watson now lives in Toledo, Ohio, with her husband and two children.